I am your friend

a book of hope

Billie Bacall

FUTUREDREAMS

FOR THOSE TOUCHED BY BREAST CANCER

20% of the profits of this publication will
be donated to the charity Future Dreams

First Published © 2018 by Doverlake, London
www.iamyourfriendbook.co.uk

ISBN 978-1-9993179-1-1

A catalogue record for this book is
available from the British Library.

Book design by adamhaystudio.com

FOR
E, M, Y & J

THANK YOU
Agnies Calkoen, Dr Gowri Motha & Carole Murray
for your invaluable guidance
&
Kate Rowe-Jones

preface

I know how it feels to be down, locked in an internal world of painful thoughts. Within the space of a couple of years, I experienced the sudden death of my husband, major surgery and embarked on a course of chemotherapy.

What can help the human spirit in moments like this? Sometimes just a spark, a detail, a word, an image can lift the mood. In the space of a breath it is possible to change the way you feel.

I did not plan to create this collection; rather it emerged through this period of my life. Feeling isolated and fearful I started to jot down fleeting images to cheer myself up. Recollections: an inspiring thought here, a word there, a feeling would ignite an expression from myself.

So, Dear Friend.
The purpose of this book is to help elevate your spirits in such moments. Even if only one small detail makes you smile and inspires you, then its purpose has been achieved.

London November 2018

Never give up

No matter what is going on

Never give up
Develop the heart
Be Compassionate
Not just to your friends
But to everyone
Be Compassionate

Work for Peace
In your heart
And in the World
Work for Peace
And I say again
Never give up

No matter what is going on
Never
give
up

Words attributed to His Holiness the 14th Dalai Lama

I'm just having a blip...

Blow Away The
Pain + Sadness

Gone

there

is

always

light

at

the

end

of

the

tunnel

HOPE
is the
better
option . . . . .

hope

despair

images

IT ALL

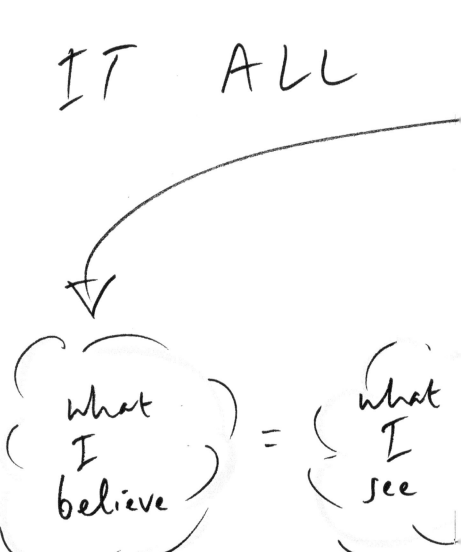

STARTS HERE

= (what I experience)

Fall
in
Love
with the
Process.

LIFE THIS WAY ⟶

GOOD TIMES

UP

DOWN

ROUGH PATCH

U Have Everything
Here To Be Happy !

life is an adventure.....

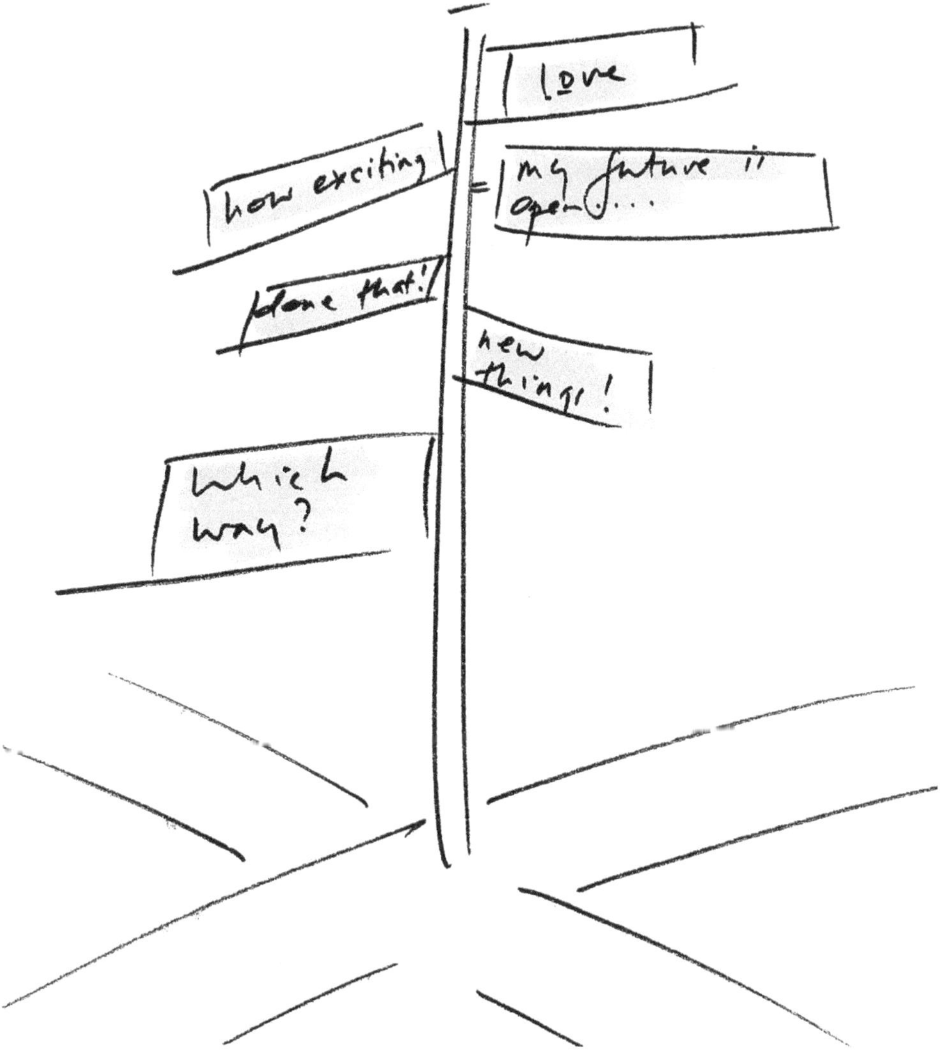

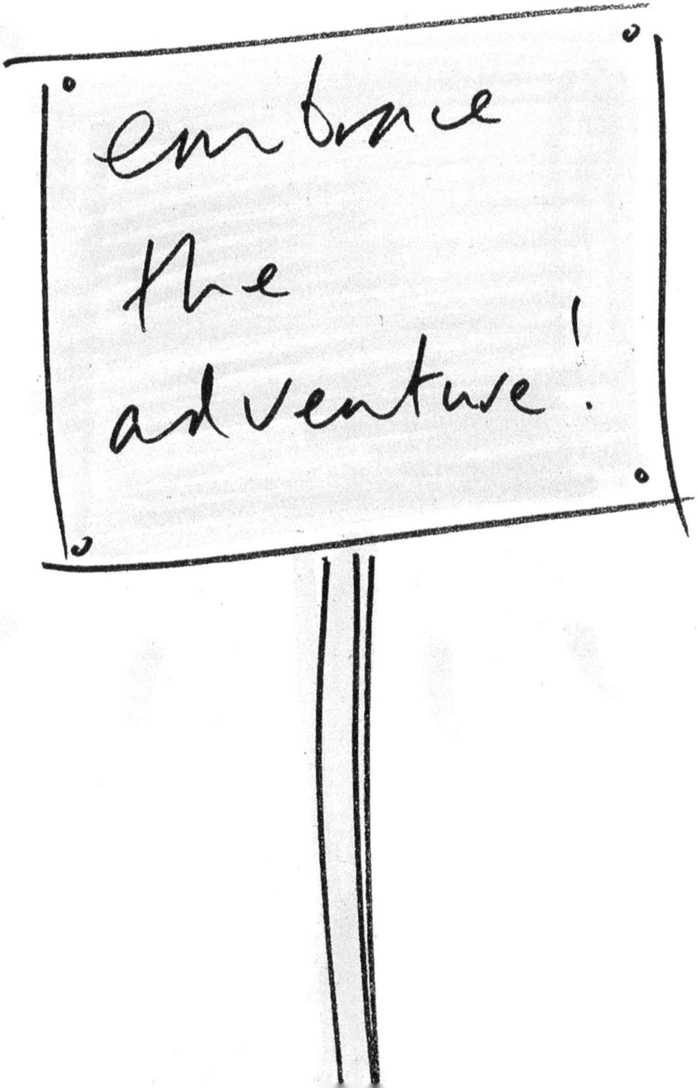
embrace
the
adventure!

direct
your inner compass

To a Beautiful
Destination !

wonderful ;

amazing things are coming my way!

Beautiful

from

the

inside!!!!!

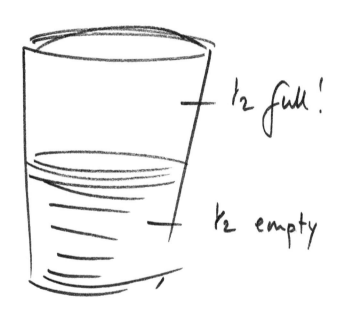

½ full!

½ empty

its how U see it......

Lets Go
For The
High Vibe !

Joy!

HIGH
VIBE

Despair

LOW
VIBE

very high vibe !!!

very very high vibe!!!

aspire to be
the
kindest
nicest
Version
of
Myself!

one) gone gone gone.

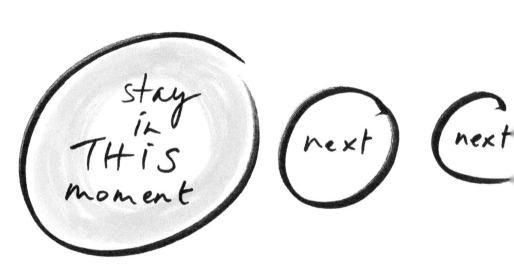

yesterday	today	tomorrow
OVER		?

TODAY

is

GOOD !

Let
It
Go....

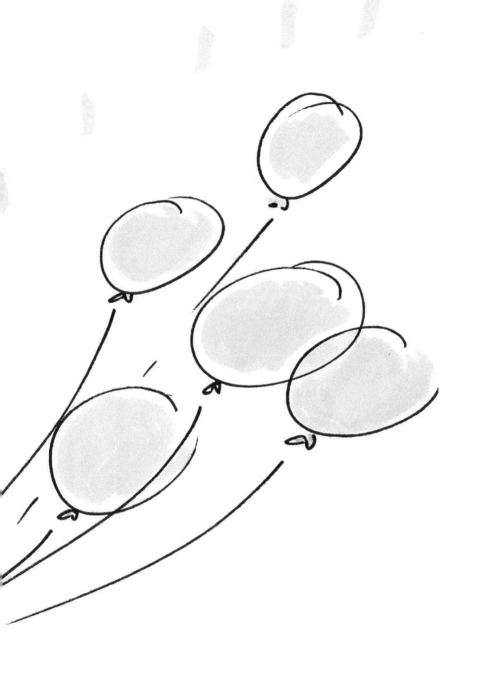

Courage
To
Go
Forward ....

Power

from

Within

Breathe
in
Courage

Simplicity

APPRECIATE

the

small pleasures

"Thank-U"

Express Gratitude Every Day!

thank-you for my wonderful life.........

- — so beautiful thank-you
- — I love you so much my friend!...
- — you are an amazing person...
- — my house is my beautiful sanctuary...
- — my family are so amazing

I LOVE my Gratitude List!!!!...

Smell
The
Sweet
Stuff !

I am at One...

with the Rythmm
of
Life !!!

I am at One....

with the Power
of the
Universe !!!

Stay connected
to those
U Love !!!

Don't be influenced by others......!!!!

Think
out
the
Box

Think Possibilities!

possibilities

<u>not</u>

~~Limitations~~

negative thought

scary thought

fear thought

sad thought

SEA OF

I can choose which thought to believe!
anxious thought
joyful thought
positive thought
THOUGHTS

.... gaze into
the darkness...

and feel
PEACE
not
fear

stay on the sunny

side of the street...

grateful
To Be
HERE !

So Happy
To Be
HERE!

humbled
to be
HERE!

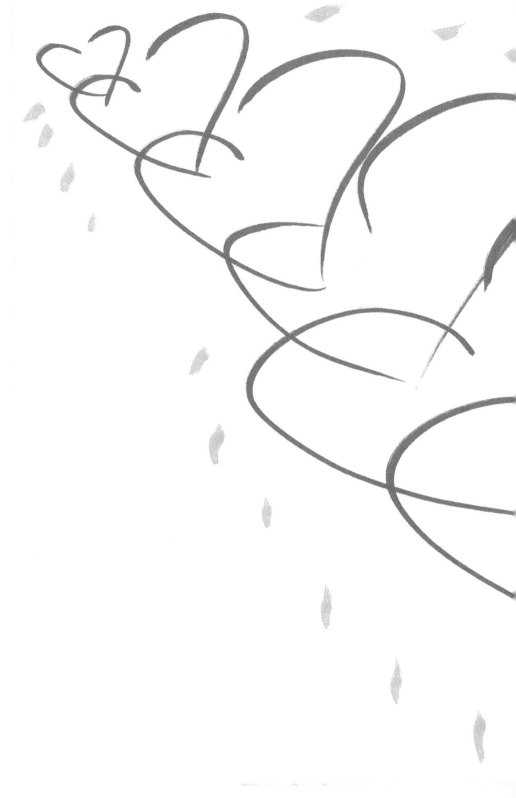

always remember...

whatever is troubling
me...

I am bigger than it.

go
dancing!

have
fun!!!....

So INTO THE
SPACE BETWEEN
2 BREATHS ...

its

beautiful

there !

flourish.

its
a
wonderful
word!

Light
positive

dark
negative

STAY ON THIS SIDE OF THE LINE!!".

horrible things
I am safe + protected!!!
worrying stuff
full on anxiety

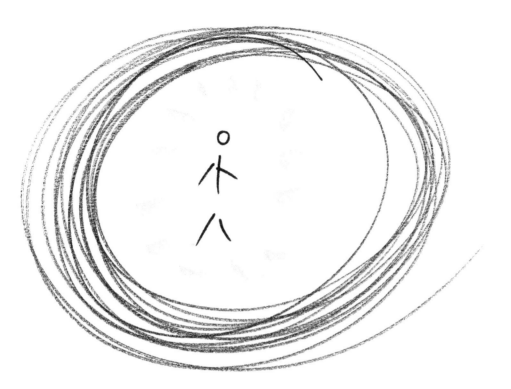

nothing
can
touch
me

say
thank
U
to your
fear

then let
it Go....

forgive
yourself

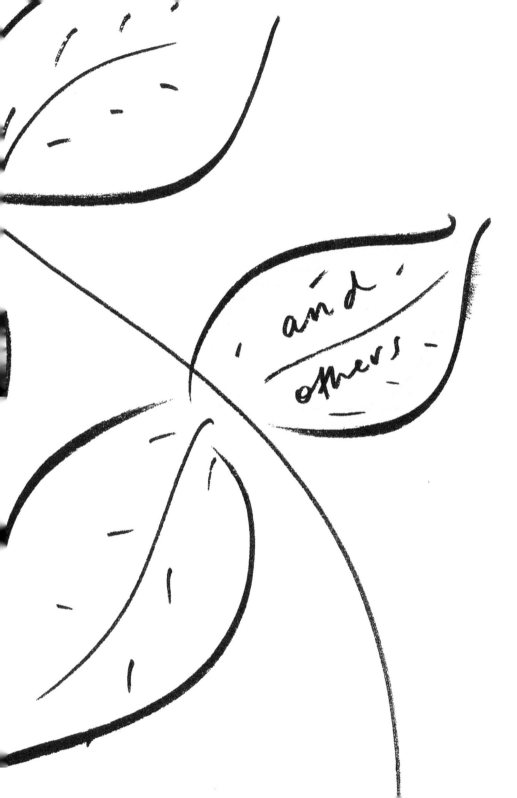

put your unhelpfull thoughts

HERE

↓

not here

↓

Joy

Knows
no
fear....

Keep
Your
Heart
Open
T. The
World . . . . .

And
To All
The

Beautiful

New

Experiences...

PARAMOUNT
MY AMAZING LIFE
STARRING
MYSELF
SOLD OUT
I want to watch THIS movie!!!!!!!

its gonna be alright
Tomorrow u will feel better
don't worry, it will all work out
No!!! . . .

it's
alright
R I S H T
now !!!...

YES!!!...

Get Rid
of the
WHAT IFS...

=

Useless
Thoughts

..... it's my choice........

Poor
Me!

I'm
Creating !!!

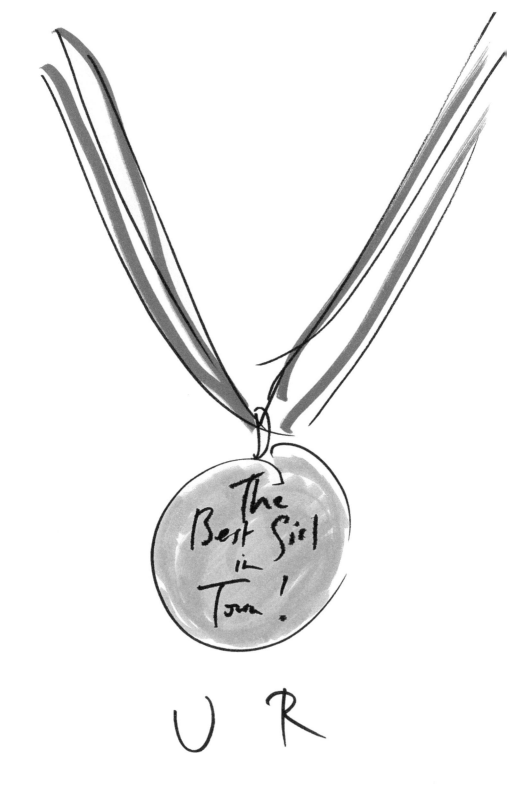

The Best!

I've
SO
done
that ....

...onto
the
next
thing...

See
Compassion
+
Kindness

as

Strengths,
not
Weaknesses

negative
self talk

→ Delete
The
Negativity
Button . . .

↓

Get Inspired !!!

stay
OPEN

~~not closed~~

no thank U.....

Take it
All . . . .
With a
Pinch of
Salt . . . .

I only see _____

OR

Boring old Apple

the beauty !

The most Beautiful
Apple in the World....

See Your Problems

as
Stepping
Stones.....

← out with the old.

IN

with

the

new

I'm
Done

With
All
That...

RISE UP

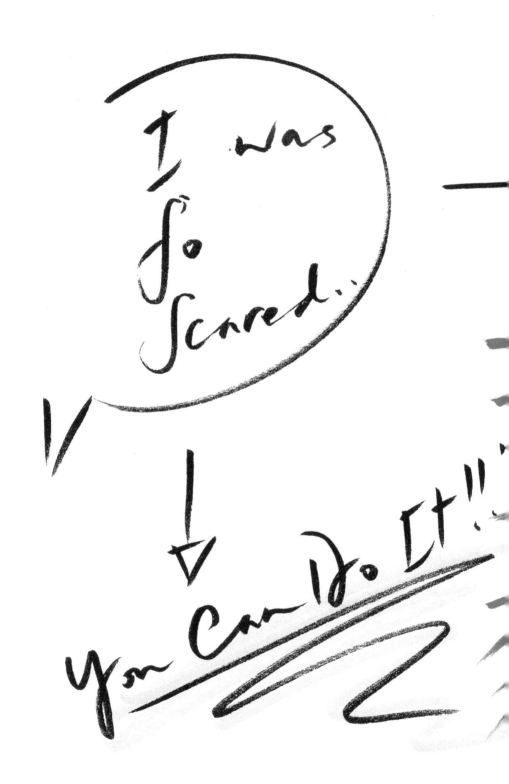

Seek
Inspiration
from
Nature

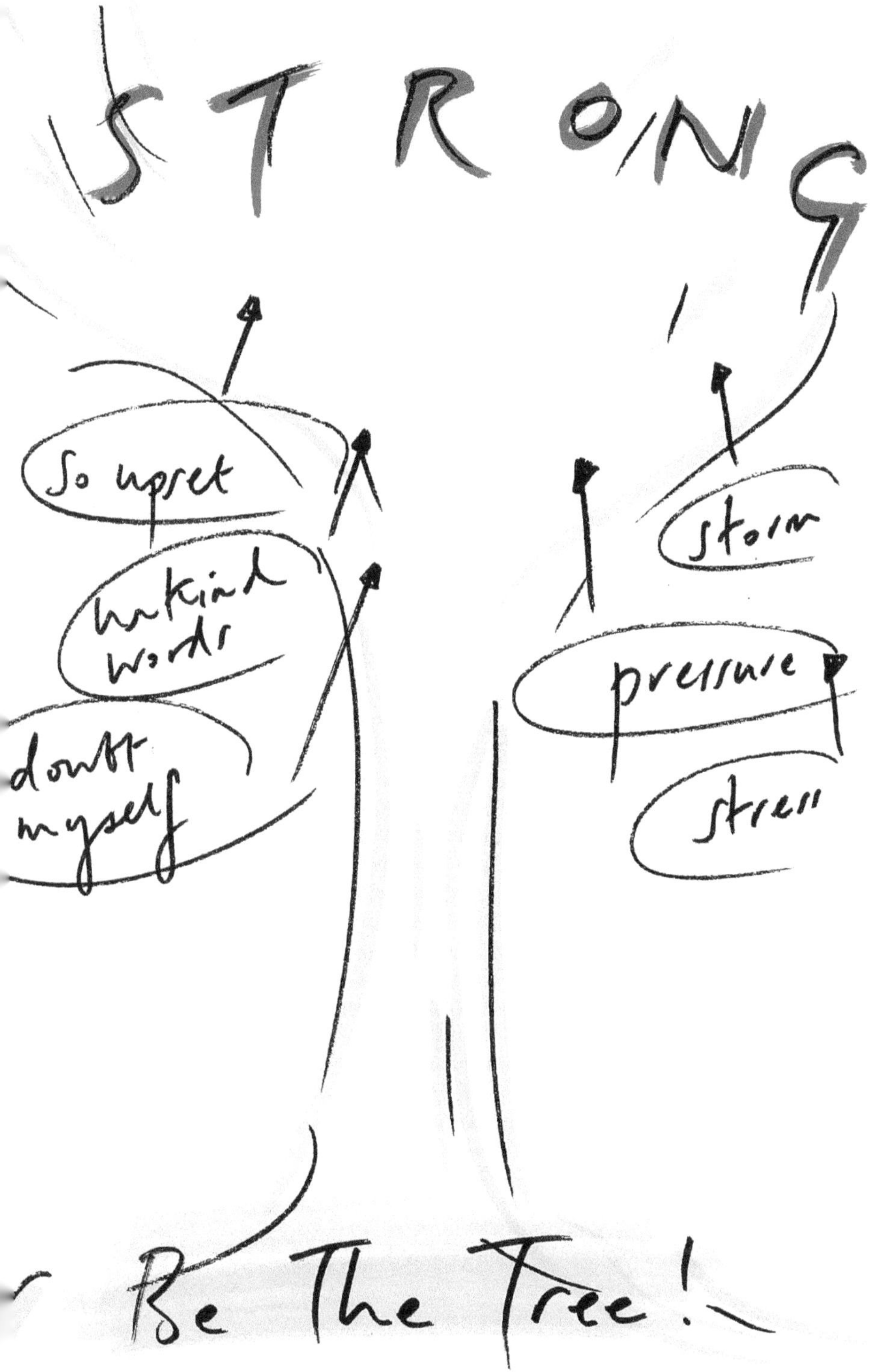
STRONG
So upset
unkind words
doubt myself
storm
pressure
stress
Be The Tree!

no
more
~~bags~~
baggage
regrets
resentments
unfinished
business

Don't
let
your
anxious
mind

peaceful   thoughts

beautiful   thoughts

peaceful   existence

beautiful   existence

Life
is
Amazing

WE ARE ALL ONE!

I don't
want to
take anymore...
I want
to
GIVE......

So

much

To

Learn

Here

Most
Important
Relationship in
Life
IS
Relationship with
Self !!!!!!!...........

DUDE!

U R

Beautiful!!!

DUDE!
U
R
Cool!!!

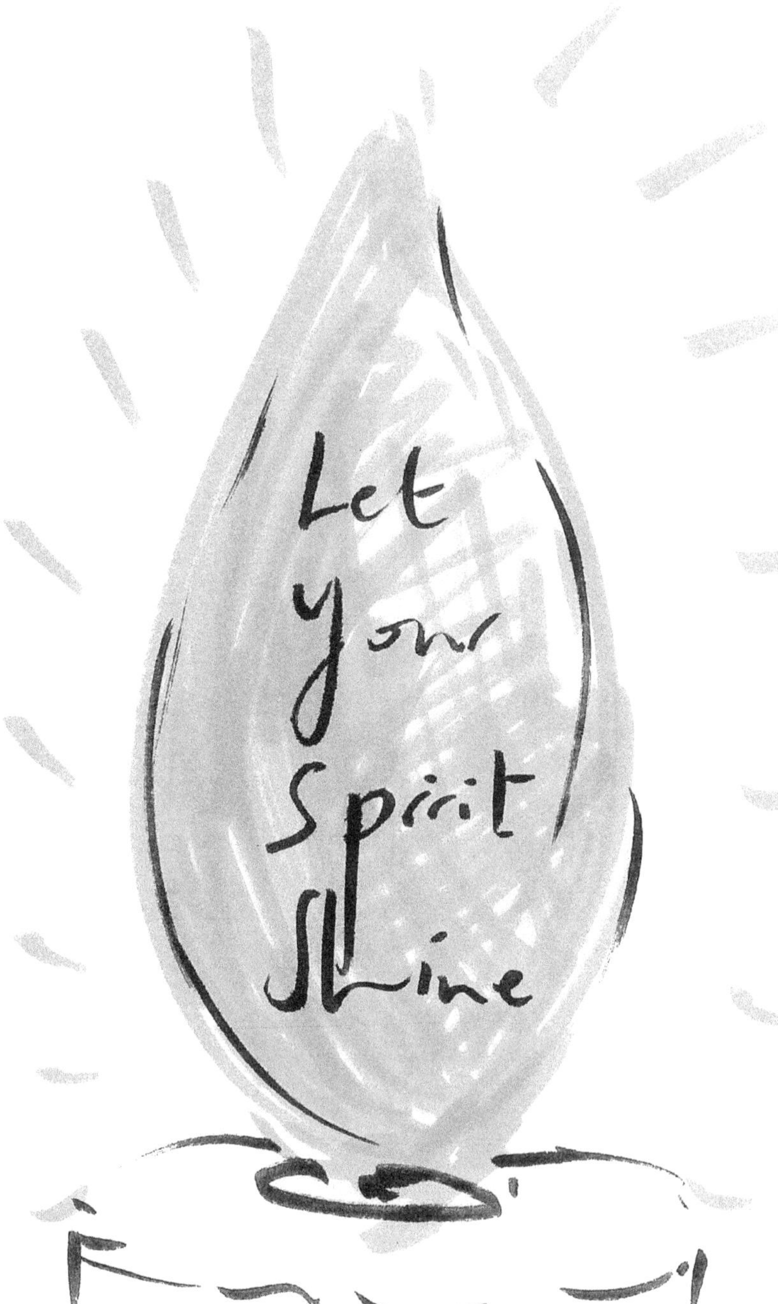
Let
your
Spirit
Shine

and become the light for all those around you

epilogue

Your beliefs become your thoughts

Your thoughts become your words

Your words become your actions

Your actions become your habits

Your habits become your values

Your values become your destiny

Words attributed to Mahatma Ghandi

inner

Find Your Way...

peace

To Create Your Own..

FUTUREDREAMS

FOR THOSE TOUCHED BY BREAST CANCER

Future Dreams was established in 2008 by mother and daughter Sylvie Henry and Danielle Leslie, when by a cruel twist of fate they were both diagnosed with breast cancer. Tragically, both women lost their lives to the disease within a year of each other in 2009. Their dream was to make sure that nobody should ever have to face this illness on their own.

Future Dreams pledges funds towards the charity's three divisions: support, awareness and research, focusing on secondary breast cancer. Working closely with Breast Cancer Haven to fund vital support centres; with Breast Cancer Care to promote awareness; and with Breast Cancer Now to fund specific research projects toward the goal that by 2050, everyone diagnosed will live.

20% of the profits of this publication will be donated to Future Dreams – www.futuredreams.org.uk